The American Flag

ELAINE LANDAU

Children's Press®
A Division of Scholastic Inc.
New York Toronto London Auckland Sydney
Mexico City New Delhi Hong Kong
Danbury, Connecticut

Content Consultant

David R. Smith, PhD

Academic Adviser and Adjunct Assistant Professor of History

University of Michigan–Ann Arbor

Reading Consultant

Cecilia Minden-Cupp, PhD

Early Literacy Consultant and Author

Library of Congress Cataloging-in-Publication Data

Landau, Elaine.
The American flag / by Elaine Landau.
    p. cm.—(A true book)
Includes bibliographical references and index.
ISBN-13: 978-0-531-12625-7 (lib. bdg.)   978-0-531-14775-7 (pbk.)
ISBN-10: 0-531-12625-0 (lib. bdg.)   0-531-14775-4 (pbk.)
1. Flags—United States—History—Juvenile literature. I. Title. II. Series.
CR113.L26 2007
929.9'2—dc22   2007005622

All rights reserved. Published in 2008 by Children's Press, an imprint of Scholastic Inc. Published simultaneously in Canada. Printed in the United States of America.
SCHOLASTIC, CHILDREN'S PRESS, A TRUE BOOK, and associated logos are trademarks and/or registered trademarks of Scholastic Inc.
1 2 3 4 5 6 7 8 9 10 R 17 16 15 14 13 12 11 10 09 08

Find the Truth!

Everything you are about to read is true *except* for one of the sentences on this page.

Which one is **TRUE**?

T or F   Betsy Ross designed the first official U.S. flag for George Washington.

T or F   A high school student designed the current U.S. flag.

Find the answer in this book.

Contents

THE **BIG** TRUTH!

Congress declared Independence Day as a federal holiday in 1870.

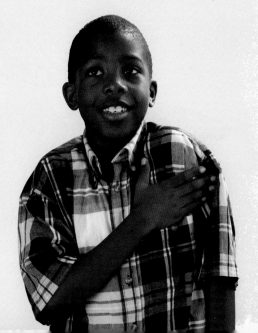

Three firefighters raise the flag at the site of the terrorist attacks on the World Trade Center in New York on September 11, 2001.

CHAPTER 1

Proudly It Waves

Some of the first American flags had no stars!

You can see the American flag all around you. It waves from flagpoles in front of a school. It flies at your local post office. Maybe your family has a flag hanging outside your house. Towns across the country turn red, white, and blue on Memorial Day, the Fourth of July, and other national holidays.

Before there was an official U.S. flag, some flew this "navy jack" flag with a rattlesnake picture. The U.S. Navy still uses this flag.

The flag is an important **symbol**. It represents the United States of America. To millions of people, the United States is a land of freedom and justice. The flag has come to symbolize these ideals.

The Statue of Liberty is another American symbol of freedom.

Flags in Battle

Soldiers have carried the American flag into battle for more than 200 years. The sight of the flag on the battlefield gives troops courage. It reminds them of what they're fighting for.

After 35 days of battle, U.S. Marines raised the flag on a hill in Iwo Jima, Japan.

The American flag can also stand for victory. One famous World War II photograph appeared in newspapers across the country. It showed U.S. Marines raising the flag after a tough battle on the island of Iwo Jima, Japan, in 1945. Many soldiers died, but the flag was a signal that others would keep fighting to win the war.

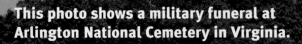
This photo shows a military funeral at Arlington National Cemetery in Virginia.

The flag honors soldiers who have died, too. A flag is laid over a soldier's coffin at a funeral. Then a member of the U.S. Armed Forces folds and presents that flag to the soldier's family. For the family, the flag is a symbol of their loved one's service to the nation.

Ends of the Earth

Americans have taken the flag to some faraway places. In 1909, American explorers Robert E. Peary and Matthew Henson brought the flag to the North Pole. Then in 1928, the American flag flew at the other end of the globe. Admiral Richard E. Byrd raised the flag at his camp in Antarctica, near the South Pole. He named the camp Little America.

This photo is of Admiral Richard E. Byrd (left) returning to Little America, Antarctica, with scientists in 1956.

Out of This World

The flag took what may have been its most exciting trip in 1969. American astronauts put a U.S. flag on the moon! Brave and daring Americans are proud to take the flag wherever they go.

There's no wind on the moon, so this flag was made to look like it is waving.

In 1969, American astronauts planted a flag on the moon. The flag has wires in it to give it a wavy shape.

A Model Flag

Some countries have used the American flag as a model for their own flags. The colors and designs mean different things to the people of each country.

Chilean flag

The white star stands for the honor of the country.

Malaysian flag

The blue square stands for the unity of the Malaysian people.

Liberian flag

The red and white stripes stand for the courage and goodness of Liberia. The blue square is a symbol for Africa.

Puerto Rican flag

The white star represents the island of Puerto Rico. The red stripes stand for blood spilled in battle. The white stripes are a symbol of peace.

In this illustration, a U.S. soldier raises the flag after a victory over the British in 1783. The British flag is shown falling to the ground.

CHAPTER 2

The Flag's History

Britain and America were enemies in the Revolutionary War, but their flags shared the colors red, white, and blue.

The United States of America started out as **colonies** in the early 1600s. The **colonists** were ruled by Great Britain. By the middle of the 1700s, the colonists no longer wanted to follow British laws or pay British taxes. But King George III of England, was not willing to let go of the colonies. Americans would have to fight for their freedom in the **Revolutionary War**.

Carrying a Flag

Americans formed an army to fight in the Revolutionary War. The new army needed a flag to carry into battle. Colonel Christopher Gadsden designed a flag in 1775. It was bright yellow with a rattlesnake in the center. The rattlesnake warned the British, "Don't Tread on Me."

Rattlesnakes are found only in the Americas. They became symbols of American courage in the Revolutionary War.

DONT TREAD ON ME

The Grand Union Flag was first flown on New Year's Day, 1776, near George Washington's army headquarters outside Boston, Massachusetts.

The colonists used other flags during the early days of the Revolutionary War. General George Washington liked the design of the Grand Union Flag. It used the same colors as the British flag. It had 13 red and white stripes as a symbol of the 13 colonies. A small version of the British flag was in the upper left corner. This part of the flag is called a **canton**.

Why would American leaders include their enemy's flag this way? At that time, some colonists still hoped they could fix things with Great Britain.

The First Official U.S. Flag

Though the war with Britain was still raging, the United States declared its independence in 1776. Americans wanted a powerful symbol of their freedom. They got one the following year. The U.S. government passed a resolution describing the first official U.S. flag.

American Flag Timeline

1777
The new U.S. government passes the Flag Act on June 14. The Stars and Stripes becomes the first official U.S. flag.

1814
The flag inspires Francis Scott Key to write "The Star-Spangled Banner."

This flag is often called the Stars and Stripes. Like the earlier Grand Union flag, it had 13 red and white stripes for the colonies.

This is the Stars and Stripes flag. The 13 stars stood for the 13 colonies.

1892

Francis Bellamy writes the Pledge of Allegiance.

1942

Congress passes the Flag Code to explain how to care for the flag.

The Story Behind the Stars and Stripes

Who made the first American flag? For years, people thought it was a **seamstress** from Philadelphia, Pennyslvania, named Betsy Ross. A famous story says Ross sewed the flag in 1776 after Washington came to her shop and gave her a sketch. Some say she even helped with the design.

But Washington was fighting with the army in New York at the time. Ross did sew other kinds of flags for the navy, but there is no proof she helped with the first official American flag.

A colonial leader named Francis Hopkinson probably created the first official flag. Historians found a copy of a bill Hopkinson sent to the government for designing "the flag of the United States" and other work. This seems to prove that he deserves the credit. But no one is completely sure.

This painting shows Betsy Ross (standing) sewing the first American flag. This popular story is now believed to be false.

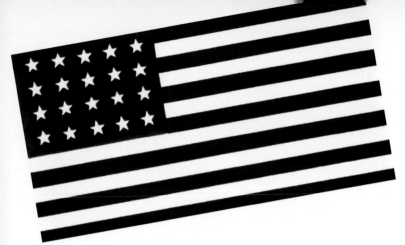

The Road to 50 Stars

After the Revolutionary War, new states began to join the **Union**. Vermont became the 14th state in 1791. Kentucky joined in 1792. Two stripes and two stars were added for these states.

There were 20 states in the Union by 1818. Government leaders realized it was not practical to keep adding red and white stripes for each new state. Congress passed a law in 1818 to return to the 13-stripe design. A star would be added for each new state. As the United States grew, it continued to add stars until there were 50.

An A+ Project

Did you know that a 17-year-old boy from Ohio designed our current flag? Robert G. Heft turned in the design for a class project in 1958. Two more states were about to enter the Union. The country needed a new flag with more stars. Heft arranged 50 stars in alternating rows of six and four stars each.

Heft gave his design to his congressman. The president's team picked his design out of almost 2,000 choices. On July 4, 1960, Heft's design was approved.

Robert G. Heft received a B- grade from his teacher for his flag design.

This photo is of Robert G. Heft in 2005 with the original flag he designed. He keeps the flag at his home in Thomas Township, Michigan.

23

The Changing Flag

The flag has changed many times over the years. Here's how.

The Gadsden Flag

(1775–1777) Colonel Christopher Gadsden uses this rattlesnake flag to lead colonists into battle.

Grand Union Flag

(1776–1777) George Washington flies a red-and-white-striped flag on January 1, 1776. The British flag, also called the Union Jack, is in the top-left corner.

The Stars and Stripes, or the 13-Star Flag

(1777–1795) The first official U.S. flag has 13 red and white stripes. The canton is made up of 13 white stars set against a blue background.

The Star-Spangled Banner, or the 15-Star Flag

(1795–1818) Two stars and two stripes are added to the flag in 1795. They represent Vermont, which joined the Union in 1791, and Kentucky, which joined in 1792.

The 48-Star Flag

(1912–1959) In 1912, President William H. Taft orders the stars to appear in six rows of eight. He also orders that all stars have a single point upward. Before this, flag makers arranged the stars as they liked.

The current U.S. Flag, or 50-Star Flag

(1959–present) In 1959, President Dwight D. Eisenhower orders that two stars be added for the last two states—Alaska and Hawaii. The country has flown this flag ever since.

A vexillologist inspects a flag that was carried into battle during the Revolutionary War. The flag was auctioned off for $11 million.

CHAPTER 3

A Glorious Banner

A vexillologist (VEK-se-LOL-o-jist) is an expert on the history of flags.

You may have heard the American flag called by different names. It is sometimes known as Old Glory or the Star-Spangled Banner. There are interesting stories behind these nicknames. Each of them shows how Americans feel about their flag.

A young girl waves American flags during a Fourth of July parade.

27

A Star-Spangled Story

American lawyer Francis Scott Key wrote the words to our national **anthem**, "The Star-Spangled Banner." At the time, the United States was fighting Great Britain in the War of 1812.

Key was being held on a British ship off the coast of Maryland on the morning of September 13, 1814. Other British ships began to fire on a nearby fort, called Fort McHenry. If the British captured this fort, they could easily control the city of Baltimore, Maryland.

British ships fire cannons on Fort McHenry.

Francis Scott Key was held aboard a British ship called the HMS *Surprise*. Why? Key may have overheard the British plan to attack Baltimore.

Key watched the attack from a British ship in the harbor. He heard the British cannon fire. He also saw what he later described as "the rocket's red glare." At dawn the next day, Key saw that the American flag was still flying over the fort. At that moment, he knew the Americans had won. The sight of the flag filled Key with joy.

Francis Scott Key wrote a poem about the experience. In the poem, he called the flag the Star-Spangled Banner. The poem was later set to music and became the U.S. national anthem.

The Story Behind Old Glory

William Driver was a ship captain from Salem, Massachusetts. In 1831, his friends gave him an American flag. Driver loved the gift and named it Old Glory. He carried it with him for the rest of his life.

In 1861, Driver was living in Nashville, Tennessee. At that time, the issue of slavery was tearing apart the United States. The Northern and Southern states were fighting each other in the Civil War. The South wanted to form its own country. Most people in Nashville didn't want the Stars and Stripes as their flag anymore. But Driver held on to Old Glory. He sewed the flag into his bed to keep it safe.

Northern soldiers captured Nashville in 1862. The soldiers and Driver flew Old Glory over the state capitol. They wanted to show that Tennessee was part of the United States again.

After a while, Old Glory became a nickname for any American flag. Many people liked the story of how Driver loved his flag and his country. Today, the original Old Glory is still being honored. The flag is on display in Washington, D.C.

This painting shows the Battle of Vicksburg. This Civil War battle took place in 1863. Northern soldiers carry the flag.

At the inauguration of President Bill Clinton, two 13-star flags, two 25-star flags, and the current flag were all displayed on the U.S. Capitol. The 25th star was added in 1836 when Arkansas, Clinton's home state, joined the Union.

CHAPTER 4

Caring for the Flag

You can buy a flag that has flown over the Capitol by contacting your U.S. senator or representative.

Did you know that the United States has rules about how to care for the American flag? These rules are called the Flag Code. The code tells us how to display the stars and stripes properly. It explains how to show respect for the flag. The United States adopted the Flag Code in 1942.

The flag should never touch the ground.

33

Flag Dos and Don'ts

There are many things to keep in mind when you display an American flag. You should not fly a flag in bad weather unless it is an all-weather flag.

If a flag is ever flown during the night, make sure proper lighting surrounds it. You should raise an American flag quickly and lower it carefully. Never let the flag touch the floor or ground.

Displaying a flag upside down means you are in serious danger.

When a ship is in trouble, sailors turn the ship's flag upside down. Anyone who sees it knows that the sailors need help.

The U.S. Flag Code states that it is customary for the flag to be taken down at sunset.

You can wear clothes that have a design similar to the U.S. flag. But an actual flag is not supposed to be made into clothing, bedding, or curtains. A picture of the flag should not be printed on paper napkins, boxes, or anything else that will be thrown away.

If a flag is torn or faded, it should be destroyed in a respectful manner. How? By burning it. Burning a flag is more respectful than tossing it in the trash. But it must be done safely by adults.

A flag is flown at half-mast on the anniversary of the September 11, 2001 attacks in New York City.

A flag is flown halfway up a flagpole as a sign of respect for the dead.

Making Flags

About 20 million flags are sold each year.
Sometimes people are especially eager to show
national pride. As many as 100 million flags are
sold during some years!

Some flags are printed on white fabric.
Other flags are made with huge sewing machines.
The stripes and blue square are stitched together.
Then stars are sewn onto the square.

A long time ago, flags were made from cotton.
Today, many are nylon, a man-made substance that
helps flags last longer—and allows them to be flown
in bad weather if they are
all-weather flags.

**This photo shows a woman sewing
in a New Jersey flag factory.**

This giant flag is part of the Memorial Day celebration in River Forest, Illinois, in 2006.

CHAPTER 5

Pledging Allegiance

The largest American flag ever made weighed 3,000 pounds!

Do you ever wonder why you say the **Pledge of Allegiance**? When you repeat those words, you are making a promise to respect the flag and be faithful to your country. This special promise dates back more than 100 years.

The U.S. Flag Code has a rule for reciting the Pledge of Allegiance. In part, it says that people should place their right hand over their heart.

39

The First Pledge

A group of schoolchildren pledge allegiance to the flag in Hampton, Virginia, around 1900.

Francis Bellamy wrote the first version of the pledge in 1892. He was working at a popular children's magazine called *Youth's Companion*. The magazine was planning a large event to celebrate Christopher Columbus's arrival in the Americas 400 years earlier. As part of the program, Bellamy wrote a short, **patriotic** speech that began with the words, "I pledge allegiance . . . ."

More than 60,000 public schools across the country took part in the celebration on October 12. More than 12 million students said the Pledge of Allegiance that day.

A Meaningful Tradition

The words to today's Pledge of Allegiance are similar to the words that Bellamy wrote, though they have changed slightly over time. To say the pledge, place your right hand over your heart, face the flag and recite: "I pledge Allegiance to the Flag of the United States of America, and to the **Republic** for which it stands, one Nation under God, **indivisible**, with liberty and justice for all."

These refugees from World War II in Europe learn the pledge after arriving safely in the United States.

Did you ever think about what the words to the pledge actually mean? When you say the Pledge of Allegiance, you give your word that you'll respect the flag and the ideas behind it. Many Americans have worked to achieve the idea of "liberty and justice for all." As long as Americans keep their promise to the flag, the country will be indivisible. That means it is not possible to break it apart. ★

When the Senate and House of Representatives meet together, they begin the session by reciting the Pledge of Allegiance.

U.S. government approves its first official flag on: June 14, 1777

Number of stars on the current U.S. flag: 50

Number of stripes on the current U.S. flag: 13

Where the American flag has been: The flag was at the North Pole (1909), Antarctica (1928), Mount Everest (1963), the Moon (1969)

Number of times the design of the U.S. flag has been changed: 26 (for 27 total versions)

Flag Day: June 14

Date the Pledge of Allegiance was written: September 1892

The Flag's Nicknames: The Star-Spangled Banner, Old Glory, the Stars and Stripes

Did you find the truth?

(F) Betsy Ross designed the first official U.S. flag for George Washington.

(T) A high school student designed the current U.S. flag.

Resources

Books

Britton, Tamara L. *The American Flag*. Edina, MN: ABDO Publications, 2003.

Ferry, Joseph. *The American Flag*. Philadelphia: Mason Crest, 2003.

Hess, Debra. *The American Flag*. New York: Benchmark Books, 2004.

Jango-Cohen, Judith. *The American Flag*. Minneapolis: Lerner Publications, 2004.

Landau, Elaine. *The National Anthem*. Danbury, CT: Children's Press, 2008.

Lloyd, Douglas G. *The American Flag*. Danbury, CT: Children's Press, 2003.

Rubin, Susan Goldman. *Flag with Fifty-Six Stars*. New York: Holiday House, 2005.

Thomson, Sarah L., Bob Dacey (illustrator), and Debra Bandelin (illustrator). *Stars and Stripes: The Story of the American Flag*. New York: HarperCollins, 2003.

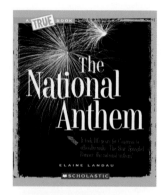

Organizations and Web Sites

Ben's Guide to U.S. Government for Kids—Symbols of U.S. Government: The Flag

http://bensguide.gpo.gov/3-5/symbols/flag.html

Learn more about the history of the flag.

Encyclopedia Smithsonian—Facts About the United States Flag

www.si.edu/Encyclopedia_SI/nmah/flag.htm

See a timeline that shows how the flag has changed.

Places to Visit

The Betsy Ross House

239 Arch Street
Philadelphia, PA 19106
215-686-1252
www.betsyrosshouse.org
Visit the house of America's most famous flagmaker.

The Flag House & Star-Spangled Banner Museum

844 East Pratt Street
Baltimore, MD 21202
410-837-1793
www.flaghouse.org

Fort McHenry National Monument and Historic Shrine

2400 East Fort Avenue
Baltimore, MD 21230
410-962-4290
www.nps.gov/fomc/
Visit the birthplace of the U.S. national anthem.

Important Words

anthem – a song that expresses praise or loyalty

canton (CAN-tuhn) – the top left section of a flag

colonies – lands settled and ruled by people from another country

colonists – people who live in a newly settled area ruled by another country

indivisible (in-duh-VI-zuh-buhl) – unable to be broken apart

patriotic (PAY-tree-AW-tik) – showing pride in and love for one's country

Pledge of Allegiance (PLEJ UHV uh-LEE-junss) – a spoken promise of loyalty to the flag and the country

republic – a country in which the people vote for their leaders

Revolutionary War – a war from 1775 to 1783 that gave the 13 American colonies independence from Great Britain, forming the United States of America

seamstress – a woman who sews for a living

symbol (SIM-bul) – an object that stands for something else

Union (YOON-yuhn) – the United States of America, especially during the Civil War

Index

About the Author

Award-winning author Elaine Landau has written more than 300 books for children and young adults. She worked as a newspaper reporter, a children's book editor, and a youth services librarian before becoming a full-time writer.

Ms. Landau lives in Miami, Florida, with her husband and their son, Michael. She enjoys writing about history and often visits the places she writes about. You can visit her at her Web site: www.elainelandau.com.